KEMET AND OTHER ANCIENT AFRICAN CIVILIZATIONS SELECTED REFERENCES

KEMET AND OTHER ANCIENT AFRICAN CIVILIZATIONS

SELECTED REFERENCES

compiled by
Vivian Verdell Gordon
Ph.D.

WTP
THIRD WORLD PRESS
CHICAGO, ILLINOIS

First Edition ISBN: 0-88378-149-2

Manufactured in the United States of America
Third World Press • Chicago
7524 S. Cottage Grove Avenue
P.O. Box 730
Chicago, IL 60619

Cover design: KENNETH ALLEN
Book design: SERIF, Ltd. - typeface: BENGUIAT

FOREWORD

Dr. Gordon has provided a vital service to both researchers and to lay scholars who are interested in the Ancient history of African people. She has pulled together and synthesized references from a variety of sources making them available in a format that is accessible to all. This service is long overdue and should stimulate further efforts to expand the pool of material that must be consulted as we attempt to reconstruct the truth of the African experience.

To assist the reader, I have indicated with an asterisk (*) those references which I think are especially important to those with limited backgrounds. I congratulate Third World Press for their recognition of the need for this resource.

Asa G. Hilliard III
Georgia State University
Atlanta, Georgia

INTRODUCTION AND ACKNOWLEDGMENTS

The references listed here provide information about ancient African civilizations. These selections are based upon recommended readings and bibliographic references by leading scholars in the field. This bibliography has been prepared in response to numerous requests by those who wish to read and to establish personal libraries about *Kemet* and other Ancient African Civilizations.

Primarily, the references listed are readily available for purchase or through local public and university libraries. However, in some instances reference has been made to books or articles that are out of print or which may be difficult to obtain. In those instances, the references have been included because of their classic importance to the contemporary research. This bibliography is not presumed to be all-inclusive. However, effort has been made to list the major publications that provide information upon which a *Black Kemet* can be documented.

I was first introduced to readings about *Kemet* and Ancient African Civilizations by Dr. Maulana Karenga, Dr. Jacob Carruthers and others who initiated the Association for the Study of Classical African Civilizations. Like so many, prior to that association, I had read with excitement the contributions by many distinguished scholars, such as Dr. John Henrik Clarke, Dr. Josef Ben-Jochannan, and Dr. Ivan Van Sertima, but it was the ASCAC interaction which provided the motivation for additional reading.

Clearly, I am an amateur in the study of Ancient African Civilizations. Because of my search for topical references, I became aware of the need for this major compilation of references. If I have not included a significant source which you believe should be listed, please write to me so that it can be included in future editions.

The compilation of this bibliography has been tedious and I am especially indebted to Dr. Asa G. Hilliard, III, for his assistance through recommendations from his extensive bibliography. Dr. Hilliard, the Fuller E. Calloway Professor of Urban Education at Georgia State University, is among those African-centered scholars who have conducted research about *Kemet* and other Ancient African Civilizations. Dr. Hilliard has identified many of the references of particular importance by an asterick (*).

I hope that this bibliography will be of practical assistance to those who have experienced difficulty identifying references on this topic, as well as those who are anxious to extend their personal libraries. I wish to express my appreciation to Black bookstores and distributors who have made many of these publications readily available to the African American community.

Vivian Verdell Gordon
Department of African
and African American Studies
The State University of New York
at Albany

KEMET AND OTHER ANCIENT AFRICAN CIVILIZATIONS SELECTED READINGS

ADAMS, William. *The Nubia Corridor to Africa.* London: Penguin Books, 1977.

ADDAI-SEBO, Akyaaba and Ansel WONG, eds. *Our Story: A Handbook of African History and Contemporary Issues.* London: The Central Race Relations Unit, Haringey Council, Civil Centre and the Association of London Authority, 1988.

ALDRED, C. *Egypt to the End of the Old Kingdom.* New York: McGraw-Hill, 1965.

———. *Art In Ancient Egypt.* Alec Tiranti, 1969.

ALDRIDGE, Cyril. *Egypt to the End of the Old Kingdom.* New York: Thomas and Hudson Publishers, 1988.

ALEXANDER, Curtis E. *African Historical Religions: A Conceptual and Ethical Foundation for Western Religions.* New York: ECA Associates, 1984.

ARKELL, A.J. *Early Khartoum: An Account of the Excavation of an Early Occupation Site.* London, 1949.

ALLEN, Thomas. *The Book of the Dead or Going Forth by Day.* Chicago: University of Chicago Press, 1974.

BAINES, J. and J. MALEK. *Atlas of Ancient Egypt.* Oxford: Phaidon Press, 1980.*

BATTISCOMBE, G. Gunn. *The Instruction of Ptahhotep.* London, 1909.

BAUMGARTEL, E. *The Cultures of Prehistoric Egypt.* Oxford University Press, 1955.

BEARDSLEY, Grace. *The Negro In Greek and Roman Civilizations, A Study of the Ethiopian Type.* London, 1929.

BEGG, E. *The Cult of the Black Virgin.* Boston: Arkana, 1985.*

BEN-JOCHANNAN, Yosef A.A. *Africa: Mother of "Western Civilization."* Baltimore: Black Classic Press.*

———. *Black Man of the Nile and His Family.* New York: Alkebu-lan Books, 1981.*

———. *African Origins of the Major Western Religions.* Baltimore: Black Classic Press.

———. *Mysteries System.* (Inquire with the above publisher.) Yosef A.A. K. Webb, and H. Brooks.

———. *Africa: The Land, The People, The Culture.* New York: W.H. Sadlier Company, 1969.*

———. *Our Black Seminarians and Black Clergy Without a Black Theology. New York: Alkebu-lan Books, 1978.*

BERNAL, Martin. Black Athena. The Afroasiatic Roots of Classical Civilization. Volume 1. The Fabrication of Ancient Greece, 1785-1985. New Brunswick: Rutgers University Press, 1987.*

———. *The Olmec World.* Berkeley: University of California Press, 1976.

BEVAN, J. *Egypt and the Egyptians: Their History, Antiquities, Language, Religion and Influence Over Palestine and Neighboring Countries.* London: George Allen & Sons, 1909.

Bonwick, James. *Egyptian Belief and Modern Thought.* London: The African Publication Society, 1983.

BRADLEY, T.A. *The Reception of the Egyptian Cults by the Greeks (330-30 BC). The University of Missouri Studies: A Quarterly of Research.* v. 10, no. 1, 1935.*

BREASTED, James H. *A History of Egypt: From the Earliest Time to the Persian Conquest.* New York: Charles Scribner & Sons, 1912. Several volumes.

———. *Ancient Records of Egypt: From the Earliest Times to the Persian Conquest.* New York: Russell and Russell Publishers, 1962. Several volumes.

———. *Egyptian Servant Statutes.* New York: Pantheon Press, 1948.

———. *The Dawn of Conscience.* New York: Charles Scribner, 1978.

BRENT, P. *Black Nile: Mungo Park and the Search For the Niger.* New York: Gordon Cremonesi, 1977.

BROWDER, Anthony T. *From the Browder File: 22 Essays on the African American Experience.* Washington: The Institute of Karmic Guidance, 1989.

BRUNSON, James E. *Black Jade. African Presence in the Ancient East.* DeKalb: Kara Publishers, 1985.

BRYAN, Cyril. *Ancient Egyptian Medicine; The Papyrus Ebers.* Chicago: Ares Publishers, Inc.

BUDGE, E.A. Wallis. *The Egyptian Book of the Dead.* New York: Citadel Press, 1990.

———. *A History of Ethiopia, Nubia and Abyssinia.* London, 1928.

———. *Annals of the Niubian Kings, With a Sketch of the History of the Nubian Kingdom of Napata.* London, 1912.

———. *Egyptian Hieroglyphic Dictionary.*

———. *Egyptian Language.*

———. *The Gods of the Egyptians.*

———. *Herb-Doctors and Physicians in the Ancient World. The Divine Origin of the Craft of the Herbalist.*

———. *Osiris and the Egyptian Resurrection.*

———. *The Queen of Sheba and Her Only Son Menyelek.* London, 1922.

———. *The Rosetta Stone in the British Museum.* London: The Religious Tract Society, 1929.

CAMAX, C.N.B. *Imhotep To Harvey: Background of Medical History.* Boston: Longwood Press, 1977. First published, 1931.

CARNEY, David. *Man and Myth. An African Viewpoint.* New York: Vantage Press, 1988. (*Note:* This book does not reference the African Origins of the concepts. However, if the reader has that background, the book presents an excellent discussion which contributes to an understanding of the African view.)

CARNY, J. *Papers and Books In Ancient Egypt.* London: H.K. Lewis & Company, Ltd., 1947.

———. *Ancient Egyptian Religion.* New York: Hutchinsons University Library, 1952.

CARRUTHERS, Jacob H. *Essays In Ancient Egyptian Studies.* Los Angeles: University of Sankore Press, 1984.

CARY, Max and E.H. WARMINGTON. *The Ancient Explorers.* London, 1929.

CHURCHWARD, Albert. *Origin and Evolution of Freemasonry.* London: G. Allen & Unwin, 1920.

———. *Signs and Symbols of Primordial Man.* Westport: Greenwood Press, 1978.

CLARK, Leone, ed. *Through African Eyes: Cultures in Change. The African Past and The Coming of the European.* New York: Praeger Publishers, 1971.

CLARK, R.T. Rundle. *Myth and Symbol in Ancient Egypt.* London: Thames and Hudson Publishers, 1959.

COLLUM, V. C.C. *Manifold Unity: The Ancient World's Perception of the Divine Pattern of Harmony and Compassion.* London: J. Murray, 1940.

COOK, H.P. *Osiris, A Study in Myths, Mysteries, and Religion.* Chicago: Ares Publishers.

COOLEY, W.D. The Negroland of the Arabs Examined and Explained: An Inquiry Into the Early History and Geography of Central Africa. Frank Cass & Co., Ltd., 1966.

CORTEGGIANI, Jean-Pierre. *The Egypt of the Pharaohs at the Cairo Museum.* Scala Books. Distributed in the U.A. by Harper & Row. First published in English in 1987.

COX, G.O. *African Empires and Civilizations.* Washington: African Heritage Publishers, 1974.

CRAIG, Alberg M., William A. GRAHAM, Donald KAGAN, etal. *The Heritage of World Civilizations.* Volume 1, to 1600. New York: MacMillan Publishing Company, 1986.

CREED, J.M. *Egypt and the Christian Church.* In S.R. Glanville, editor, *The Legacy of Egypt.* Oxford: Clarendon Press, 1943.

DANQUAH, J.B. *Akan Laws and Customs and the Akim Abuakwa Constitution.* London: George Routledge & Sons, Ltd., 1928.

DAVID, A.R. *The Egyptian Kingdoms.* London: Elsevier Phaidon, 1975.

DAVIDSON, BASIL. *The African Genius. An Introduction to African Social and Cultural History.* Boston: Little, Brown and Company, 1969.

———. *The African Past: Chronicles From Antiquity to Modern Times.* Boston: Little, Brown and Company.

———. *Discovering Our African Heritage.* Boston: Ginn and Co., 1971.

———. *The Lost Cities of Africa.* (Revised Edition.) Boston: Little, Brown, and Company, 1959.

DAVIS, S. *Race Relations In Ancient Egypt: Greek, Egyptian, Hebrew, Roman.* New York: Philosophical Library, 1952.

DE BUCK, A., ed. *Egyptian Reading Book; Exercises and Middle Egyptian Texts.* Chicago: Ares Publishers.

DEGRAFT-JOHNSON, J.C. *African Glory. The Story of Vanished Negro Civilizations.* Baltimore: Black Classic Press, 1986.

DELUBICZA, R.A.S. *Sacred Science: King of Pharaonic Theocracy.* New York: Intertraditions, 1982.

———. *Aymavol Ns Rhw Aymvolix: Egypt, Science and the Evolution of Consciousness.* New York: Autumn Press, 1978.

———. *Egyptian Miracle: An Introduction to the Wisdom of the Temple.* Rochester, Vermont: Inner Traditions, International, Ltd., 1985.

———. *Symbol and the Symbolic: Egypt, Science and the Evolution of Consciousness.* New York: Autumn Press, 1978.

DIOP, Cheikh Anta. *The African Origin of Civilization: Myth or Reality.* Westport, Connecticut: Lawrence Hill & Company, 1974, 1978.*

———. *The Cultural Unity of Black Africa.* Chicago: Third World Press, 1978.*

———. *Origin of the Ancient Egyptians.* In Mokhtar, G., *General History of Africa II: Ancient Civilizations of Africa.* Berkeley: University of California Press, 1981, pp. 7-57.*

———. *Report on the Symposium on "The Peopling of Ancient Egypt and the Deciphering of the Meroitic Script."* Cairo, January 28 - February 3, 1974.*

DOANE, T.W. *Bible Myths and Their Parallels in the World's Major Religions: Being a Comparison for the Old and New Testament Myths and Miracles With Those of Heathen Nations of Antiquity, Considering Also Their Origins and Meaning.* New York: Truth Seeker Press, 1948. First published 1882.

DOBLHOFER, E. *Voices In Stone: The Decipherment of Ancient Scripts and Writings.* New York: Collier, 1971.

DOW, S. *The Egyptian Cults in Athens. Harvard Theological Review,* V. 30, pp. 183-232, 1937.

DROWER, M. *Nubia: A Drowning Land.* New York: Atheneum Press, 1970.

DUBOIS, F. *Timbuktu The Mysterious.* New York: Henry Holt & Company, 1939.

DUBOIS, W.E.B. *Black Folk Then and Now.* New York: Henry Holt and Company, 1939.

———. *The World and Africa.* New York: Viking Press, (1946) 1968.

DUNHAM, Dows. *The Royal Cemetaries of Kush.* Cambridge: Cambridge University Press, 1950.

EDWARDS, I.E.S. *The Early Dynastic Period In Egypt.* Cambridge: Cambridge University Press, 1964.

Egypt's Golden Age: The Art of Living in the New Kingdom, 1558-1085. Catalogue of the Exhibition. Museum of Fine Arts, Boston, 1982.

EL-AMIN, Mustafa. *Freemasonry: Ancient Egypt and the Islamic Destiny.* Jersey City: New Mind Productions, 1989.

EMERY, Walter B. *Lost Land Emerging.* New York: Charles Scribner, 1967.

———. *Nubian Treasure.* London: Methuen Press. 1948.

ERMAN, Adolf. *The Literature of the Ancient Egyptians.* London: Methuen Press, 1927.

———. *A Handbook of Egyptian Religion.* London: The African Publication Society, 1981. First published 1907.

ERSKINE, Beatrice Stuart. *Vanished Cities of Northern Africa.* London: Hutchinson & Company, 1927.

EVANS, A.J. *The Palace of Minos: A Comparative Account of the Successive Stages of the Early Cretan Civilizations As Illustrated by the Discoveries of Knossos.* London, 1921-1935.

———. *The Early Nilotic, Libyan and Egyptian Relations with Minoan Crete.* London, 1925.

FAGE, J.F. and R.A. OLIVER. *Papers In African Prehistory.* Cambridge: The University Press, 1979.

FARNELL, L.R. *The Cults of the Greek States.* V. III, Oxford University Press, 1907.

FAZZINI, R.A. *Art From the Age of Akhenaten.* Brooklyn: The Brooklyn Museum Press, 1970.

FELL, B. *American BC: Ancient Settlers in the New World.* Wallaby Press, 1976.

FRANKFORD, Henry, ed. *Before Philosophy.* London: Harmondsworth Press, 1949.

———. *Kingship and the Gods. A Study of Ancient Near Eastern Religion and the Integration of Society and Nature.* Chicago: University of Chicago Press, 1978.

———. *The Birth of Civilization in the Near East.* New York: Doubleday, 1956.

FRANKFORD, Henry. (ed.). *Before Philosophy.* London, Harmondsworth Press, 1949.

———. *The Intellectual Adventure of Ancient Man: An Essay On Speculative Thought in the Ancient Near East.* Chicago: University of Chicago Press, 1977.

FREUD, S. *Moses and Monotheism.* New York: Vintage Press, 1967.

GARDINER, Alan. *Egypt of the Pharaohs.* London: Oxford University Press, 1980.

GARSTANG, John, ed. *Meroe, The City of the Ethiopians.* Oxford University Press, Clarendon Press, 1911.

GILLINGS, Richard J. *Mathematics in the Time of the Pharaohs.* New York: Dover Publications, 1972.

GLANVILLE, S.R.K., ed. *The Legacy of Egypt.* Oxford: The Clarendon Press, 1942.

GRAFTON, E.S. *The Ancient Egyptians and the Origin of Civilization.* Freeport, New York: Books for Libraries Press, 1967.

GRAVES, K. *The World's Sixteen Crucified Saviors: Christianity Before Christ.* New York, Truth Seeker Press, 1975. First published 1875.*

GRAVES, Robert and Raphael PATAI. *Hebrew Myths; The Book of Genesis.* Garden City: Doubleday Press, 1964.

GRIFFITH, F.L. *Meroitic Inscriptions, Napata To Philae.* London, 1912.

GRIULE, M. *Conversations With Ogotemmeli: An Introduction To Dogon Religious Ideas.* Oxford University Press, 1972.

HALL, Harry R. *The Ancient History of the Near East.* Methuen Press, 1913.

HALL, Manley P. *Free Masonry of the Ancient Egyptians.* Los Angeles: Philosophical Research Society, Inc., 1971.

———. *Secret Teachings of All Ages.* Los Angeles: Philosophical Research Society, 1978.

HANSBERRY William Leo. *Sources for the Study of Ethiopian History.* Washington: Howard University Press, 1931.

———. *Africa and Africans As Seen By Classical Writers.* Washington: Howard University Press, 1977.

———. *Pillars In Ethiopian History.* Washington: Howard University Press, 1974.

HARRIS, Joseph E. *Africans and Their History. The African Presence In Asia: Consequences of the East African Slave Trade.* Washington: Howard University Press, 1974.

HARRIS, Joseph E., ed. *Africa and Africans As Seen By Classical Writers: The William Leo Hansberry African History Notebook.* Volume II. Washington: Howard University Press, 1977.*

HARRIS, Joseph E. and E.F. WENTE. *An X-Ray Atlas of the Royal Mummies.* Chicago: University of Chicago Press, 1980.

HASKINS, R.W. *The Arts, Sciences and Civilizations, Anterior To Greece and Rome.* Buffalo: A.W. Wilgus, 1844.

HEEREN, A.H. L. *Historical Researches Into the Politices Intercourse, and Trade of the Principal Nations of Antiquity.* Oxford University Press, 1834.

HERODOTUS. *The History of Herodotus.* New York: Tudor Publishing Company, 1939.

HEYOB, S.K. and M.J. VERMASEREN. *The Cult of Isis Among Women In the Greco-Roman World.* E.J. Brill, 1975.

HICKS, R.I. *Egyptian Elements In Greek Mythology. Transactions of the American Philosophical Association,* XCIII, pp. 106-107, 1962.

HIGGINS, G. *Anacalypsis: An Attempt To Draw Aside the Veil of the Saitic Isis: Or An Inquiry Into the Origin of Languages, Nations and Religions.* London, Onngman, Rees, Oras, Brown, Green, Paternoster Row, 1972.

HILLIARD, A.B. *Kemet Concepts In Education.* In *Nile Valley Civilizations, Journal of African Civilizations* Ltd. Edited by I. Van Sertima. 1985, pp. 153-162.

HILLIARD, Asa G., ed. *The Teachings of Ptahhotep, The Oldest Book In the World.* First published circa 2388 B.C. to 2356 B.C., First Kemetic (Egyptian) Dynasty. Atlanta: Georgia, Blackwood Press.

HOFFMAN, M.A. *Egypt Before the Pharaohs: The Prehistoric Foundations of Egyptian Civilizations.* New York: Alfred Knopf, 1979.

HOFFMEIER, J.K. and E.S. MELTZER, eds. *Egyptological Miscellanies.* Chicago: Ares Publishers, Inc.

HOLTZOLAW, R.F. *The Saints Go Marching In: A One Volume Hagiography of Africans, Or Descendents of Africans Who Have Been Cannonized By the Church Including Three of the Early Popes.* Shaker Heights: The Keeble Press, 1980.

HOSKINS, G.A. *The Travels In Ethiopia, Above the Second Cataract of the Nile.* London, 1914.

HOUSTON, Drusilla D. *The Wonderful Ethiopians and the Ancient Cushite Empire.* Baltimore: Black Classic Press.*

HUGGINS, Willis N. and John G. JACKSON. *An Introduction To African Civilizations: Main Currents In Ethiopian History.* New York: W.W. Norton Co., 1976.

HULL, R.W. *African Cities and Towns Before the European Conquest.* New York: W.W. Norton Co., 1976.

HURRY, Jamieson B., M.D. *Imhotep, The Egyptian God of Medicine.* Chicago: Ares Publishers, Inc. 1987.

HUTCHINSON, L.D. *Out of Africa: From West Africa Kingdoms To Colonization.* Washington: Smithsonian Institution Press, 1979.

IBRAHIM-HILMY. *The Literature of Egypt and the Soudan From the Earliest Times to the Years 1885.* London: Trubner Publication, 1986-87.

IDOWU, E.B. *African Traditional Religion: A Definition.* New York: Orbis Books, 1975.

IONS, V. *Egyptian Mythology.* London, Hamlyn: 1965.

IVERSEN, E. *The Myth of Egypt and Its Hieroglyphics In European Tradition.* Copenhagen, Gad., 1961.

JACKSON, B.D. *We Are the Children of the Great Ancient Africas.* Brooklyn: Black News Printing by H. M. Walker, 1981.

JACKSON, John G. *Ethiopia and the Origin of Civilization. A Critical Review of the Evidence of Archaeology, Anthropology, History and Comparative Religion, According to the Most Reliable Sources and Authorities.* Baltimore: Black Classic Press.*

———. *Introduction To African Civilizations.* New Jersey: The Citadel Press, 1970.

Man, God, and Civilization. Secaucus: Citadel Press.*

———. *The Mysteries of Egypt.* Chicago: Mass Inc. 1980.

JAIRAZBHOY, R.A. *Ancient Africans and Chinese In Early America.* Totowa, New Jersey: Rowman and Littlefield, 1974.

JAMES, George G.M. *Stolen Legacy: The Greeks Were Not The Authors of Greek Philosophy, But the People of North Africa, Commonly Called the Egyptians.* San Francisco: Julian Richardson Associates. From the original, 1954.*

JENKINS, U.D. *Ancient African Religion and the African American Church.* North Carolina: Flame International, 1978.

JOHNSON, S. *The History of the Yorubas From Earliest Times to the Beginning of the British Protectorate.* Lagos, Nigeria: CSS Bookshops, 1976.

JONES, E.L. *Tutankhamon.* Seattle: Edward L. Sloan and Associates, 1978.

JULY, R.W. *A History of the African People.* New York: Charles Scribner's Sons, 1974.

KAMIL, J. *Luxor: A Guide To Ancient Thebes.* London: Longman Press, 1976.

———. *Sakkara: A Guide to the Necropolis and the Site of Memphis.* New York: Longman, 1978.

KAMUSE, K.B. *Down The Nile.* Detroit: Greater Visions, Inc. 1978.

KARENGA, Maulana. *The Husia. Sacred Wisdom of Ancient Egypt.* Los Angeles: The University of Sankore Press.

———. *Restructuring Kemetic Culture. Proceedings of the Third and Fourth ASCAC Conferences.* Los Angeles: The University of Sankore Press, 1989.*

KARENGA, Maulana, and Jacob H. CARRUTHERS. *Kemet and The African Worldview; Research and Restoration.* Los Angeles, California, The University of Sankore Press.*

KASTER, Joseph. *Life and Thought of Ancient Egypt.* New York: Holt, Rinehart & Company, 1968.

KINGSLAND, W. *The Gnosis or Ancient Wisdom In the Christian Scriptures.* Wheaton, Illinois: The Theosophical Publishing House, 1968.

KI-ZERBO, J., ed. *General History of Africa I: Methodology and Pre-History.* Berkeley: University of California Press, 1981.

KOSTLER, A. *The Thirteenth Tribe: The Khazar Empire and Its Heritage.* New York: Random House, 1976.

LAMY, L. *Egyptian Mysteries: New Light On Ancient Spiritual Knowledge.* New York: Crossroads Press, 1981.

LEAKEY, L.S.B. *By The Evidence: Memoirs 1932-1951.* New York: Harcourt Brace Janovich, 1974.

———. *The Stone Age Races of Kenya.* London: Oxford University Press, 1935.

LEPSIUS, R. *Letters From Egypt, Ethiopia and the Peninsula of Sinai.* London: Henry G. Bohn, 1853.

LESKO, B.S. *The Remarkable Women of Ancient Egypt.* Berkeley: B.C. Scribe Publications, 1978.

LESKO, Leonard H. *The Ancient Egyptian Book of Two Ways.* Berkeley: University of California Press, 1972.

LESLAU, W. *Falasha Anthology: The Black Jews of Ethiopia.* (Translated from Ethiopic sources) New York: Schocken Press, 1951.

LICHTHEIM, Mirian. *Ancient Egyptian Literature.* Berkeley: University of California Press. 1975. (*Note:* Volume 1 - The Old and Middle Kingdoms; Volume 2 - The Late Period; Volume 3 - The New Kingdom.

LITANY OF THE SUN. THE LITANY OF RA. Texts translated with commentary by Alexander Piankoff. New York: Pantheon Books, 1964.

LOST BOOKS OF THE BIBLE AND THE FORGOTTEN BOOKS OF EDEN. New York: The World Publishing Company, 1963.

LOTH, Heinrich. *Women In Ancient Africa.* Westport, Connecticut: Lawrence Hill & Company, 1987.

LUGARD, Lady. *A Tropical Dependency: An Outline of the Ancient History of the Western Sudan With An Account of the Modern Settlement of Northern Nigeria.* Frank Cass & Co., Ltd., 1964.

MACKENZIE, N. *Secret Societies.* New York: Crescent, 1967.

MACMICHAEL, H.A. *A History of the Arabs In the Sudan and Some Account of the People Who Preceded Them and of the Tribes Inhabiting Darfur.* Cambridge, 1922.

MAGIE, D. *Egyptian Deities In Asia Minor In Inscriptions and on Coins. American Journal of Archaelogy, v. 57, pp. 163-187, 1953.*

MASPERO, G. Art In Ancient Egypt. New York: Charles Scribner's Sons, 1912.

MASSEY, Gerald. *Ancient Egypt: The Light of the World.* New York: Samuel Weiser, Inc., 1970.

———. *A Book of Beginnings.* London, Williams and Norgate, 1881. New York: Samuel Weiser, Inc.*

———. *The Historical Jesus and The Mythical Christ: What Christianity Owes To Ancient Egypt.* London: Pioneer Press. (Some library copies exist.)

———. *Gerald Massey's Lectures.* New York: Samuel Weiser, Inc., 1973.

MBITI, John S. *African Religions and Philosophy.* New York: Anchor Books, 1970.

MEANS, Sterling M. *Black Egypt and Her Negro Pharaohs.* Baltimore: Black Classic Press.

MERCER, S.A. B. *Egyptian Hieroglyphic Grammar.* Chicago: Aries Publishers, 1926.

MERTZS, B. *Redland, Blackland: Daily Life In Ancient Egypt.* New York: Dodd Mead Company, 1978.

MEYEROWITZ, E. *The Divine Kingship In Ghana and Ancient Egypt.* London: Faber and Faber, 1960.

MICHALOWSKI, Kazimierz. Art of Ancient Egypt. New York: Harry N. Abrams, Inc., undated.

MOKHTAR, G. *General History of Africa II: Ancient Civilizations of Africa.* New York: United Nations Educational Scientific and Cultural Organization, 1981.

MOLDENKE, Charles, editor. *The Tale of the Two Brothers. A Fairy Tale of Ancient Egypt.* Baltimore: Maryland, Black Classic Press, 1988.

MONTET, Pierre. *Eternal Egypt.* New York: The New American Library, 1964.

———. *Rameses The Great: Everyday Life In Egypt In His Days.* Chicago: Ares Publishers, Inc.

MOOREHEAD, A. *The Blue Nile.* New York: Vintage Books, 1983.

———. *The White Nile.* New York: Vintage Books, 1983.

MORENZ, Siegfried. *Egyptian Religion.* Ithaca: Cornell University Press, 1978.

MORET, A. and G. DAVY. *From Tribe To Empire.* New York: Alfred A. Knopt.

———. *Kings and Gods of Egypt.* New York: G.P. Putnam, Inc.

MU'MIN, Ridgely Abdul. *Amen: The Secret Waters of the Great Pyramid.* Greensboro, North Carolina: A.M. Distributors, 1989.

MURRAY, Margaret A. *The Splendour That Was Egypt.* London: Sidgwick and Jackson, 1972.

Museum of Fine Arts, Boston. *Egypt's Golden Age: The Art of Living In The New Kingdom, 1558-1085 B.C.*

MYER, Isaac. *The Oldest Books in the World: An Account of the Religion, Wisdom, Philosophy, Ethics, Psychology, Manners, Proverbs, Sayings and Refinement.* New York: E.W. Dayton Company, 1900.

NASHVILLE, E.H. *The XI Dynasty Temple At Dier El-Bahari.* Boston: Egypt Exploration Fund, 1907.

NEWBERRY, P. *Ancient Egyptian Scarabs.* Chicago: Ares Publishers, Inc.

New York Times, *"Fossils Trace Man Back 600,000 Years in Gorge in Africa."* August 24, 1959.

———. *"43,000 Year Old Mine Discovered in Swaziland."* February 8, 1970.

NIGHT, G.A. F. *Nile and Jordan: Being the Archaeological and Historical Interrelations Between Egypt and Canaan From the Earliest Times to the Fall of Jerusalem.* London, 1921.

NOBLES, Wade W. *African Psychology.* Oakland: The Black Family Institute. 1987.

NOBLES, Wade W., Lawford L. GODDARD and William E. CAVIL, III. *The Km Ebit Husia. Authoritative Utterances of Exceptional Insight for the Black Family.* Oakland: The Black Family Institute Press, 1989.

OBADELE, I. and A. OBADELE. *Civilizations Before the Time of Christ.* Detroit: The House of Songhay, 1975.

OESTERLEY, W.O. E. *The Wisdom of Egypt and the Old Testament.* New York: MacMillan & Company, 1927.

O'LEARY, D. *The Coptic Church and Egyptian Monasticism.* In Glanville, ed., *The Legacy of Egypt.* Oxford: Clarendon Press, 1943.

OLELA, Henry. *From Ancient African To Ancient Greece: An Introduction to the History of Philosophy.* Atlanta: The Black Heritage Corporation, 1981.

OLIVER, R. and C. OLIVER, eds. *Africa In the Days of Exploration.* New Jersey: Prentice Hall, 1965.

OSEI, G.K. *The African: His Antecedents, His Genius and His Destiny.* New York: University Books, 1971.

———. *African Contributions To Civilization.* London: The African Publication Society, 1973.

———. *A Short History of West Africa A.D. 1000 to the Present.* New York: Hill and Wang, 1973.

OTTO, Eberhard. *Ancient Egyptian Art.* New York: Harry N. Abrams, Inc.

PARKER, G.W. *The Children of the Sun.* The Hamitic Language of the World, 1918.

PERRY, W.J. *The Children of the Sun. A Study in the Early History of Civilization.* New York: E.P. Dutton & Company, 1923.

PETRIE, William. *Egypt and Israel.* Society for Promoting Christian Knowledge, 1912.

———. *A History of Egypt.* London: Methuen, 1924.

———. *A History of Egypt During the XVII and XVIII Dynasties.* Freeport: Books for Library Press, 1972.

———. *Hykson and Israelite Cities.* London: School of Archaeology, 1906.

———. *The Pyramids and Temples of Gizeh.* London: Field and Tuer.

———. *Religious Life In Ancient Egypt.* New York: Cooper Square Publishers, 1972.

———. *Religion and Conscience In Ancient Egypt.* New York: Arnold Press, 1980.

PHILLIPSON, D.W. *African Archeology.* Cambridge: Cambridge University Press, 1985.

———. *"The search for early man."* *National Geographic,* 168(5), 1985.

POLITEYAN, J. *Biblican Discoveries In Egypt, Palestine, and Mesopotamia.* London: C.J. Thyme, 1921.

POLITT, J.J. *The Egyptian Gods In Attica: Some Epigraphical Evidence.* Hesperia, v. 34, pp. 125-130, 1965.

POOLE, S.F. *The Moors In Spain.* London: G.P. Putnam and Son, 1899.*

PORTMAN, I. *A Guide to the Temples of Philae.* Cairo: The Palm Press, 1984.

POSNER, G. *Dictionary of Egyptian Civilization.* New York: Tudor Publishing Co., 1962.

Pyramid Texts. *The Pyramid Texts In Translation and Commentary By Samuel A.B. Mercer.* New York: Longmans, 1952.

QUATTLEBAIUM, M.C. *Niger Is Really Black. Blacks, Browns, Burnt-Faces Throughout Holy Writ.* Sarasota, Florida: Lindsay Curtis Publishing Company, 1984.

RAPOPORT, L. *The Lost Jews: The Last of the Ethiopian Falasha.* New York: Stein and Day, 1980.

RASHIDI, R., ed. *African Presence In Early Asia. Special Issue: Journal of African Civilization,* 1985.*

RAWLINSON, G. *Ancient Egypt.* New York: G.P. Putnam's Sons, 1986.

REDFORD, D.B. *History and Chronology of the Eighteenth Dynasty of Egypt. Seven Studies.* Toronto: University of Toronto Press, 1925.

REISNER, G.A. Excavations At Kerma. Cambridge, Massachusetts, 1923.

REED, B. *Regel In the Soul: A Sacred Text of Ancient Egypt.* Translated. New York: Intertraditions Press, 1978.

RIEFSTAHIAL, Elizabeth. *Thebes In the Time of Amunhotep III.* The University of Oklahoma Press, 1964.

ROBINSON, C.S. *The Pharaohs of the Bondage and the Exodus.* New York: The Century Co., 1887.

ROGERS, J.A. *From "Superman" to Man.* St. Petersburg, Florida: Helga Rogers, 1989.

———. *Nature Knows No Color Line: Research Into the Negro Ancestry in the White Race.* New York: Helga M. Rogers, 1952.*

———. *Africa's Gift To America.* New York: Helga M. Rogers, 1956.*

———. *Sex and Race.* New York: Helga M. Rogers, 1944.*

———. *The Real Facts About Ethiopia.* Atlanta: The Atlanta Center, Atlanta University, 1982.

World's Great Men of Color. Riverside, New Jersey: MacMillan Publishing Co.

ROULLET, A. *The Egyptian and Egyptianizing Monuments of Imperial Rome.* Leiden, E.J. Brill, 1972.

SAAD, E. *Social History of Timbuktu: The Role of Muslim Scholars and Notables, 1400-1900.* Cambridge: Cambridge University Press, 1983.

SAMEH, Waley-el-dine. *Daily Life In Ancient Egypt.* New York: McGraw-Hill, 1964.

SAVE-SODERBERGH, Torgny. *Pharoahs and Mortals.* London: Robert Hall, Ltd., 1961.

SCHURE, Edouard. *The Great Initiates: A Study of the Secret History of Religions.* New York: Multimedia Publishing Company, 1977.

SCHWALLER, De Lubicz. *Egyptian Miracle. An Introduction to the Wisdom of the Temple.* Rochester, Vermont: Inner Traditions, Ltd., 1985.

———. *"Chick-Pea" The Living Face of Ancient Egypt.* Rochester, Vermont: Inner Traditions, Ltd.

———. *Her-Bak Egyptian Initiate.* Rochester, Vermont: Inner Traditions, Ltd., 1956.

———. *Living Face of Ancient Egypt.* Rochester, Vermont: Inner Traditions, Ltd.

———. *Opening of the Way.* Vermont: Inner Traditions, Ltd.

———. *Sacred Science: The King of Pharaonic Theocracy.* Rochester, Vermont: Inner Traditions, Ltd.

———. *Symbols and The Symbolic: Ancient Egypt, Science and the Evolution of Consciousness.* Rochester, Vermont: Inner Traditions, Ltd.

SEIFERT, Charles. *The Negro's or Ethiopian's Contribution to Art.* Baltimore: Black Classic Press.

SELIGMAN, C.G. *Egypt and Negro Africa: A Study In Divine Kingship.* London: George Rutledge & Sons, Ltd., 1934.

SETI, F.O. and H. El ZEINI. *Abydos: Holy City of Ancient Egypt.* Los Angeles: L.L. Company, 1981.

SIMPSON, William E., ed. *The Literature of Ancient Egypt.* New Haven: Yale University Press, 1972.

SMITH, G. Elliot. *The Influence of Ancient Egyptian Civilization In the East and In America.* Victoria University of Manchester, 1983.

SNOWDEN, Frank M. *Blacks In Antiquity: Ethiopians In the Greco-Roman Experience.* Cambridge: Harvard Press, 1970. (An excellent reference on the given topic. However this author does *not* support a Black Kemet.)

SOLMSEN, F. *Isis Among the Greeks and Romans.* Cambridge: Harvard University Press, 1979.

SPENSE. *The Mysteries of Egypt or the Secret Rites and Traditions of the Nile.* London: The African Publication Society, 1929.

ST. CLAIR, George. *Creation Records Discovered In Egypt: Studies In the Book of the Dead.* London: David Nutt, 1898.

STEINDORFF, G. and K.C. Steele. *When Egypt Ruled the East.* Chicago: University of Chicago Press, 1957

STEWART, Desmond, et.al. *The Pyramids and Sphinx.* New York: Newsweek Book Division, *Newsweek,* 1971.

STIERLIN, Henri. *The World of the Pharaohs.* New York: Sunflower Press, 1978.

SUGDEN, E.H. *Israel's Debt To Egypt.* London, 1928. Reprinted by the African Publication Society, London, 1983.

SWEETING, Earl and Lez EDMOND. *African History: An Illustrated Handbook.* London Strategic Policy Unit. Race Equality Policy Group, 1988.

SWEETMAN, David. *Women Leaders In African History.* London: Heinemann Education Books, 1984.

TANNER, Benjamin Tucker. *The Negro In Holy Writ.* Philadelphia, 1902. (Library copies.)

TARHARKA. *Black Manhood: The Building of Civilization By the Black Man of the Nile.* Washington, D.C.: The University Press of America, 1979.

TEMPLE, R.K.G. *The Sirius Mystery.* New York: St. Martins Press, 1976.*

THOMPKINS, Peter. *Secrets of the Great Pyramid. The Mystery of the Great Pyramid of Cheops.* New York: Harper & Row, 1971.

———. *The Magic of Obelisks.* New York: Harper & Row, 1981.

THOMSON, Arthur and D.R. MacIVER. *The Ancient Races of the Thebaid: Being an Anthropometrical Study of the Inhabitants of Upper Egypt From the Earliest Prehistoric Times to the Mohammedan Conquest.* Oxford University Press, 1905.

THOMPSON, R.F. *The Four Moments of the Sun: Congo Art In Two Worlds.* Washington, D.C.: National Gallery of Art, 1981.

ULLENDORFF, E. *Ethiopia and the Bible: The Schweich Lectures, 1967.* London: Oxford Universty Press, 1968.

UNESCO. *The Peopling of Ancient Egypt and the Deciphering of Meroitic Script. Proceedings of the Symposium Held In Cairo From 28 January to 3 February 1974.* New York: The United Nations, 1975.*

VAN SERTIMA, Ivan, ed. *African Presence In Early Europe.* New Brunswick: Transaction Books, 1986.

———. *They Came Before Columbus, The African Presence In America.* New York: Random House, 1976.*

———. *Egypt.* Rutgers University, *Journal of African Civilizations,* 1980.*

———. *Egypt Revisited. Journal of African Civilizations.* Reprint Volume 4, No. 2. Rutgers University, November, 1982.*

———. *Nile Valley Civilizations. Proceedings of the Nile Valley Conference, Atlanta.* September 26-30, 1984. Morehouse College, Atlanta, Georgia, 1989.*

VERMASEREN, M.J. and S.K. HEYOB. *The Cult of Isis Among Women In the Greco-Roman World.* Leydan, E.J. Brill, 1975.*

VOLNEY, C.F. *The Ruins of Meditation on the Revolutions of Empires: And the Law of Nature.* New York: Truth Seeker Company, 1950. First published 1793.

VON WUTHENAU, Alexander. *Unexpected Faces In Ancient America: 1500 B.C. to 1500 A.D., The Historical Testimony of Pre-Columbian Artists.* New York: Crown Publishers, 1975.

WADDELL, W.G. *Manetho.* Translated. Cambridge: Harvard University Press, 1980.

WAINWRIGHT, G.A. *The Sky-Religion In Egypt: Its Antiquity and Effects.* Westport, Conn.: Greenwood Press, 1971.

WALSH, M. *The Ancient Black Christians.* San Francisco: Julian Richardson, 1969.

WEATHERWAX, J.M. *The African Contribution: Parts I and II.* Los Angeles: The John Henry and Mry L. Dunn Bryant Foundation, 1968.

WEAVER, K.F. *"The Search for our Ancestors." National Geographic.* 168(5), 560, 1985.*

WEIGALL, Arthur. *The Life and Times of Akhenaton.* London: Thornton-Butterworth, 1923.

WELLRD. *Lost World of Africa.* New York: E.P. Dutton, 1967.

WEST, J.A. *Serpent In the Sky: The High Wisdom of Ancient Egypt.* New York: Harper and Row, 1979.

WHITE, Jon Manchip. *Everyday Life In Ancient Egypt.* New York: Dorset Press, 1963.

———. *Ancient Egypt Anthropology.* New York: Dorset Press.

———. *Ancient Egypt: Its Cultures and History.* New York: Dover Publications. 1970.

WEINER, L. *Africa and the Discovery of America.* New York: Kraus Reprint Company, 1971. First published 1920.

WILDUNG, D. *Egyptian Saints: Deification In Pharaonic Egypt.* New York: New York University Press, 1977.

WILLIAMS, B. *The Lost Pharaohs of Nubia.* In *Nile Valley Civilizations. Journal of African Civilizations Ltd.,* Inc., 1985.

WILLIAMS, B. *The Lost Pharaohs of Nubia.* In *Nile Valley Civilizations. Journal of African Civilizations Ltd,* Inc., 1985.

WILLIAMS, Chancellor. *The Destruction of Black Civilization. Great Issues of a Race From 4500 B.C. To 2000 A.D.* Chicago: Third World Press, 1987, 1989.*

WILSON, John A. *The Culture of Ancient.* Chicago: University of Chicago Press, 1951.

WINDSOR, Rudolph R. *From Babylon To Timbuktu. A History of The Ancient Black Races Including the Black Hebrews.* Smithtown, New York: Exposition Press, 1982.

WINLOCH, H.E. *The Rise and Fall of the Middle Kingdom In Thebes.* New York: MacMillan, 1947.

WOODSON, Carter G. *The African Background.* Washington, D.C.: ASALAH, 1936.